CHAPLAINS OF ANZAC

—— New Zealand's fallen Chaplains of the Great War ——

CHAPLAINS OF ANZAC

—— New Zealand's fallen Chaplains of the Great War ——

CHAPLAINS ROGER LANG

&

DR. JENNIFER BETHAM-LANG

langbookpublishing.com

Cover design by Blair McLean

National Library of New Zealand Cataloguing-in-Publication Data
Lang Book Publishing 2015

ISBN 978-0-9941176-5-6 - Paperback
ISBN 978-0-9941248-4-5 - Hardback
eISBN 978-0-9941250-0-2 - eBook
eISBN 978-0-9941250-2-6 - ePub

Published in New Zealand
A catalogue record for this book is available from the National Library of New Zealand.
Kei te pātengi raraunga o Te Puna Mātauranga o Aotearoa te whakarārangi o tēnei pukapuka.

ACKNOWLEDGEMENTS

Lang Book Publishing, Limited would like to thank Dr. Jena Webb for her contribution to academia and researching this book.

Named after a Napoleonic battle, Jena Webb has military history in her blood. She received her Ph.D. in English (2012) and an M.A. in Medieval Studies (2007) from the National University of Ireland, Galway. Her work is interdisciplinary, focusing on how language and literature represent historical periods. She is currently preparing for an M.A. in Military History, with an emphasis on WWI, in 2015. She presently lives in her native Central New York where she works as a freelance writer and editor.

As well, a special round of appreciation goes to all the brave women and men of the New Zealand Defence Force Chaplaincy who contributed to this book. Thanks go to:

CHAP1 Lance Lukin
CHAP2 Ants Hawes
CHAP3 Brian Fennessy
CHAP3 Chris Haines
CHAP4 Janie McPhee
CHAP4 Jimmy Ullrich
CHAP4 Ken Diekema
CHAP4 Michael Berry
CHAP3 Ra Koia
CHAP4 Russell Bone
CHAP4 Tavake Manu
CHAP4 Zane Elliot

FOREWORD

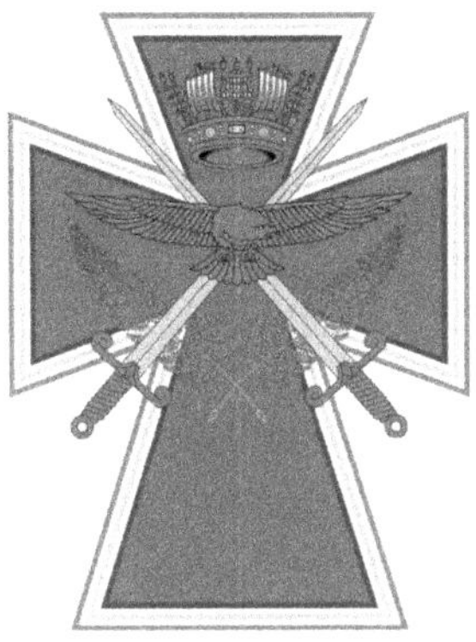

On 25 December 1814, at Oihi Bay in the Bay of Islands, the Good News of the gospel was first proclaimed in New Zealand. For over 200 years men and women of faith and courage have continued to proclaim that same Good News through times of joy and celebration as well as in times of sorrow and despair. It has been proclaimed in times of peace and also in times of war. Throughout our nation's relatively short history we have experienced many periods of conflict both within New Zealand and further afield. During this time, whenever New Zealand troops have been engaged in any form of military action, chaplains have been right along side of them bringing comfort and consolation. Chaplains served both Colonial and Maori troops during the New Zealand Wars, bridging the gap between both sides and also journeyed with New Zealand troops to South Africa during the Boer War. It is no surprise then, that when New Zealand declared war on Germany in 1914, New Zealand chaplains also signed up and prepared for war.

The wonderful collection of stories in this book tell the oft time overlooked tales of the chaplains who left New Zealand and served their God, King and Country on foreign fields of battle. In all over 140 chaplains served as part of the NZEF. This book contains the stories of seven of those who paid the ultimate sacrifice.

One of these stories is that of Chaplain William Grant, the first New Zealand chaplain to die on active service. Chaplain Grant died at Hill 60, Gallipoli, while searching for fallen and wounded soldiers. By all accounts he was a wholly remarkable clergymen, a faithful chaplain, and a gifted poet. I have had the privilege to visit Hill 60, and to walk among the many New Zealand graves on the Gallipoli Peninsula. Overwhelmingly the graves mark the final resting place of the brightest and best of our nation, young men cut down in their youth. Most of them were in their early twenties. However, Chaplain Grant wasn't a young man– far from it. He died at age 56. In many ways he had every opportunity to be excused from the war, and yet he felt compelled to go so as to be with his men. Chaplain Grant left Gisborne on Sunday 16 August 1914 with the first draft of men to join the main body of the NZEF. In his farewell letter to St Andrew's Church in Gisborne, Chaplain Grant said "in view of the fact that my own future is so uncertain, and that if I can stand the rigours of the campaign I shall certainly stay with the boys until the end of the war," He knew where he needed to be, and what he needed to do – not to remain in the safety of home, but with those heading off into the uncertainty of war.

In his farewell address to the men who were about to embark for Europe he passed on this poignant message:

This is not a time for words. It is a time for deeds, and how magnificently those deeds are being done in the world to-day. From north and south and east and west, from the frozen lands and from the tropical seas, our sons are marching or sailing out to the help of the old Motherland, and to defend our possessions and our liberties. War at any time is horrible, and this war upon which we have entered is the most terrible war in all the ages, and deep damnation in the sight of God and men should be the portion of those responsible for it. That our sons and other's sons, the very flower of the manhood of Europe, should be set against one another is incredible, and one can only pray, that this war may be the end of all wars in so far as civilised and Christianised communities are concerned. But to-day we desire not to dwell upon the sadness of farewell. We want you to remember that our thoughts and our prayers will go with you, and that we shall be thinking of you and praying for you when you are on the wide sea, with its perils, and when you are on land, and when you go into the test of battle. We hope you will play the game – the game of life – that you will live clean, pure, straight, and noble lives, and if you are put into the test of battle you will so play the game that the mother who bore you, although it break her heart, will be proud of you [for]. I applaud and bow the knee to the mothers who are giving you to the Empire's call. Some of you boys who have volunteered have no idea what it is costing the mother who bore you to let you go. Yet they are letting you go while their hearts are aching and breaking. They have given you to the Empire at the cost *of sacrificial pain. See to remember that the mothers who bore you are praying and thinking of you while far away. God bless and be with you. We commend you to the care of God in Whom we trust, and pray that you will be able by His Grace so to put yourself in His keeping in the day of peril, and if death claim you – you will pass into the land of eternal daylight.*

Chaplain Grant did not live to see the end of the Great War, and while he was unable to remain with his men until the end of the war, he lies buried amongst those he went to serve – watching over them for eternity.

It has often been said that "dying for freedom isn't the worst thing that can happen: being forgotten is". This collection of stories ensures that the sacrifice of New Zealand's Anzac chaplains is not forgotten.

Well done, you good and faithful servants of God.

Chaplain Class I Lance Lukin, QHC, OStJ, JP
Principal Defence Chaplain

July 2015

CONTENTS

But war, Jock, is a hellish thing!
Oh man it gars me greet,
For mithers on the ither side
Are juist as gude an' sweet.

Their laddies haena made the war,
An' only fecht, because
Like oor ain laddies, they've been taught
Tae gaird their King an' laws.

An' deep damnation, surely, Jock,
Shall be the judgment just
On men who for their ain fause ends
This horror on us thrust.[1]

Wm. Grant
Chaplain-Major

1 The Orari Tatler: A Souvenir of the Voyage of the New Zealand Expeditionary Force from Wellington to Alexandria, no. 5 (1914, Nov. 21): 85, accessed July 3, 2015, http://goo.gl/tFRrNC

INTRODUCTION

In the summer of 1914, Europe shook with the fissures of national discontentment and imperialism. As the great empires strengthened their networks of alliances and, in effect, sowed seeds of enmity, distant nations fell victim to the lure of patriotism and the hunt for adventure. Thousands of miles away from the Old World, the satellites of the British Empire also prepared for war.

Roughly two million men enlisted from England's commonwealth. In 1914, the New Zealand Expeditionary Force had "an effective strength of 25,685 men."[2] Soon, however, students, athletes, farmers and clerks embraced the call for volunteers with the "unanimous fervour of imperial patriotism."[3] By the end of the war, over 100,000 men had enlisted in New Zealand alone.[4] This number is not remarkable in and of itself until we consider that the total population of New Zealand in 1914 was an estimated 1,089,000; thus, 9% of the country's population, all men aged 20-40, embarked on active service.[5] More than 16,000 of these men died between early August 1914 and the armistice of November 1918.[6] Another 40,000 men were wounded in the same four years.[7]

---

2 Wayne Stack, The New Zealand Expeditionary Force in World War I (London: Osprey Publishing, 2011), 7.

3 Bishop, "The Call of the Empire."

4 Patrick Bishop, "The Call of the Empire, the Call of the War," The Telegraph, December 31, 2013, accessed July 1, 2015, http://goo.gl/JvDQlN

5 "First World War by the Numbers," Ministry for Culture and Heritage, last modified September 23, 2014, accessed July 13, 2015, http://goo.gl/zvSSOj

6 Ibid. The official 1924 roll of honour lists roughly 18,058, which includes men who died during the war, but also after it from wounds, sickness, etc.

7 Statistics of the Military Effort of the British Empire during the Great War, 1914–20 (London: H. M. Stationery Office, 1922), 771.

Among these men, who were fighting and dying far from home, was the simple chaplain. Presbyterian, Catholic, Methodist: these men were humble soldiers of Christ, sent to succour the wounded and provide peace to the dying. They served in hospitals and aid stations; they walked the trenches and lingered near the front lines; they gathered the wounded from no-man's land and bivouacked with their regiments when relieved from duty. It is easy to assume that they were kept out of harm's way, but "the risk taken by chaplains [was], if anything, greater on the whole than that taken by the men who [went] right into the attack."[8] The chaplain was not equipped with gun or bayonet, and the badge of the red cross, which might have provided a modicum of safety, was not always a discernible (or discouraging) symbol on the field of battle.

The men in this collection were all chaplains. Some were Catholic, some Presbyterian, some Methodist; some were born outside New Zealand, others were descendants of British immigrants; some left behind children, a few of which the fathers would never meet. A few took part in the Dardanelles Campaign, while the others found themselves entrenched in Belgium or France. They committed themselves to the demands of battle and the needs of the men with whom they served. Each of these men volunteered to be a part of the war effort. Each of these men died for King and country.

These are the New Zealand padres of World War One.

8 "Praise for Chaplains," New Zealand Herald, November 1, 1915, accessed July 12, 2015, http://goo.gl/98HxYW

CHAPTER 1

Chaplain-Major William Grant

KIA, Hill 60, Gallipoli, 28 August 1915

William Grant Portrait, Auckland Weekly News 1915.[9]

William Grant was born in 1859 in Kirriemuir, Scotland, but emigrated with his family to Waipukurau, New Zealand in 1870. Educated in New Zealand, he studied theology at New College, Edinburgh and, at the age of 20, was ordained as a Presbyterian minister.[9] His service to the faith began at St. Andrew's Church, New Plymouth, where he remained for three years before moving on to St David's Presbyterian Church, Leeston, in 1891.[10]

It was during his fifteen-year tenure in Leeston that Grant

9 "William Grant," Auckland War Memorial Museum, accessed July 3, 2015, http://goo.gl/z47dIJ

10 Ibid.

left the greatest impression among his flock. An article in the *Ellesmere Guardian* memorialised Grant's amiability, saying, "he was a most diligent and faithful pastor, and those who had passed through seasons of sickness or bereavement would never forget his visits.[11] In 1904, he settled at St. Andrew's Church in Gisborne, where he remained until the outbreak of World War I.

As with so many men in the early stages of the war, Grant volunteered; he was the first Presbyterian chaplain to do so.[12] Upon enlisting, he was made senior chaplain in the Wellington Mounted Rifles Brigade of the Main Expeditionary Force. At the time, the Rifles consisted of roughly 550 men, including Grant.[13]

The Rifles embarked upon the SS *Orari* on 16 October 1914; it would be a part of the first transport of Australian and New Zealand troops to the Middle East and the infamous Gallipoli Campaign.[14] While on the *Orari*, Chaplain-Major Grant took it upon himself to fund and edit the "Orari Tatler," a periodical describing the men and events on the *Orari* itself as it sailed from Wellington to Alexandria.[15] Within its pages are written accounts of the fleet and the men; sketches poking fun at officers, letters from soldiers and *on dits* heard from Grant's compatriots, all of which were included to help pass the time as they sailed towards war. Two of the poems within

11 "The Late Chaplain-Major Grant," Ellesmere Guardian, April 29, 1916, accessed July 3, 2015, http://goo.gl/cCrXe0.

12 Joseph Angus Mackay, Historic Poverty Bay and the East Coast, N.I., N.Z. (Gisborne, N.Z.: J. A. Mackay, 1949), NZETC, 335-36.

13 Wilkie, 3.

14 Major A. H. Wilkie, Official War History of the Wellington Mounted Rifles Regiment 1914-1919 (Wellington, N.Z.: Whitcomb and Tombs Ltd., 1924), NZETC, chapt. 2.

15 "New Zealand at War: 1914-1918," Presbyterian Archives Research Centre, accessed July 3, 2015, http://www.archives.presbyterian.org.nz/photogallery14/page1.htm.

the serial were written by Grant himself, the first entitled "A Call of the Blood,"[16] and the second, "The Great War."[17]

The *Orari Tatler* was sold for a small fee, but was not sufficient enough to cover the printer's costs. Grant provided partial payments on the greater debt while in Egypt and promised to continue even after leaving for the front. When he died, £74 was still owed Whitehead, Morris & Co. Ltd., the Tatler's printers, located in Egypt.[18]

The men of the Wellington Mounted Rifles disembarked in Alexandria, Egypt on 3 December 1915, and took trains south to Zeitoun Camp, just outside of Cairo. Grant and the Rifles would remain in Zeitoun until May 1915; these months were filled with intense training and drills to prepare the men for battle. On 8 May 1915, the Rifles returned by train to Alexandria and then sailed as reinforcements to the Gallipoli Peninsula.[19] Major Grant arrived at Anzac Cove on 12 May aboard the HMT *Glentully Castle*, whereupon the regiment was shuttled inshore; it contained "25 officers and 451 other ranks."[20] Thereafter, the Wellington Rifles moved onto Walker's Ridge, relieving the Nelson and Deal battalions.[21]

Shortly after arriving on the peninsula, the Turks launched an attack (19 May) that would leave 13,000 of their own men wounded or dead. The Anzac losses were significantly less,

16 The Orari Tatler: A Souvenir of the Voyage of the New Zealand Expeditionary Force from Wellington to Alexandria, no. 1 (1914, Oct. 24): 15, accessed July 3, 2015, http://goo.gl/35cL2T

17 Ibid, no. 5 (1914, Nov. 21): 85-86.

18 "New Zealand at War: 1914-1918."

19 "Wellington Mounted Rifles Regiment Timeline: 1915," Ministry for Culture and Heritage, last modified September 23, 2014, http://goo.gl/YDdy0l

20 Wilkie, 15.

21 Ibid, 17.

with only "160 killed and 468 wounded."[22] Grant would likely have participated in the truce of 24 May, where both armies gathered and buried the dead that had begun to rot in the heat since the battle five days before. In a letter written by the chaplain, dated 27 June, he described the surreal experience of fighting on the peninsula:

> *The Sabbath calm that enveloped earth and sky was suddenly broken by a hurtling shell, which passed overhead and burst on the beach below. That seemed to be the signal for a general fusillade, and in the space of a few minutes we had perfect pandemonium of noise made up of rifle and gun fire. Shells were bursting on three sides of us, and one lodge in the cliff ten feet above our dining table, but no one was injured.*[23]

By the end of May, the Wellington Mounted Rifles had decreased to "24 officers and 327 other ranks."[24]

Major Grant would have witnessed countless minor skirmishes during his time along Walker's Ridge, as well as the last major offensive undertaken by Anzac forces. The Battle of Chunuk Bair, which began 5 August, provided many days of action for the Rifles. They experienced heavy fire from the Turks as they took and held Destroyer Hill, as well as Big Table Top; there were few overall losses during these attacks.[25] On 9 August, the Wellington Mounted Rifles reinforced the line at

22 "Digging in, Fighting Back: The Turkish Attack, 19 May, 1915," Gallipoli and the Anzacs, accessed July 3, 2015, http://goo.gl/D3GaHf

23 "Sunday on Gallipoli," Poverty Bay Herald, April 28, 1915, accessed July 3, 2015, http://goo.gl/hFIzjo

24 "Wellington Mounted Rifles Regiment Timeline."

25 Wilkie, 45-50.

Chunuk Bair where they experienced "10 hours [of] Ottoman ... assault ..., supported by heavy artillery, machine-gun and rifle fire. Some Allied naval gunfire "and artillery fire ... [fell] short and hit the New Zealand and British trenches."[26] The Rifles experienced heavy losses during these 24 hours, losing a total of 117 men.[27]

Through all of these periods of fighting and respite, Grant tended to the wounded, sick and dying. Moreover, he provided solace for men facing the constant barrage of bullets from the Ottoman enemy. He received no special treatment, remaining at his comrades' sides "through thick and thin, oblivious to danger, thinking only of the service that he could render."[28] He was with the Rifles as they moved north to Hill 60 on 23 August, where his regiment relieved the Canterbury Mounted Rifles.[29] He was with them when they were involved in another assault on Hill 60. Heavy machine-gun fire pinned down the Allied advance; the casualties of that day's offensive for the Rifles were more than one hundred.[30]

On 28 August 1915, Major Grant was seeing to the wounded amid the skirmishes and shellfire. While searching among his fallen comrades, Grant came upon a trench of wounded Turks, where he tended to their needs and dressed their wounds. Moving further along in search of wounded, "the ground in the vicinity ... covered with dead bodies ..., [Grant] remarked, 'We are now most assuredly in the Valley

26 "Wellington Mounted Rifles Regiment Timeline."

27 Ibid.

28 "Death of Chaplain Major Grant," Poverty Bay Herald, September 6, 1915, accessed July 3, 2015, http://goo.gl/aB65DG

29 Terry Kinloch, Echoes of Gallipoli: In the Words of New Zealand's Mounted Riflemen (New Zealand: Exisle Publishing, Ltd., 2010), 241.

30 Ibid, 242.

of the Shadow of Death,' and immediately afterwards he was killed."[31] He died instantly at the age of 56.

During his tenure as Chaplain with the Wellington Mounted Rifles, it was Grant who often wrote the dreaded letters home, informing a fallen soldier's loved ones of his bravery and sacrifice.[32] His funeral, held on 30 August 1915 upon Hill 60, was well attended,[33] as was his memorial service at St. David's Church, Leeston in April 1916.[34] He was survived by his widow, Mrs. Isabella Grant, and their five children, two of whom were fighting on the Western Front.[35] Grant was posthumously awarded the Star British War and Victory Medals for his services to the Empire.[36]

Chaplain-Major William Grant remains now on Hill 60, where his men had held their ground and fought the good fight. It is a fitting resting place for a man who did not care where he slept at night, so "long as he was with his boys."[37]

31 Wilkie, 66-67.

32 "The Late Chaplain-Major Grant."

33 "New Zealand at War: 1914-1918," Presbyterian Archives Research Centre, accessed July 3, 2015, http://goo.gl/iwCyvh

34 "The Late Chaplain-Major Grant."

35 "Death of Rev. William Grant - Killed at the Dardanelles," Poverty Bay Herald, September 6, 1915, accessed July 3, 2015, http://goo.gl/gNtmx4

36 "Grant, William - WW1 11/86 - Army [Image 1]," 13 October 1923, Archway, Archives New Zealand, http://goo.gl/L7mpA6

37 "New Zealand at War: 1914-1918."

Chaplain-Major William Grant's final resting place.

CHAPTER 2

Chaplain-Major James J. McMenamin

KIA, Messines, 8 June 1917

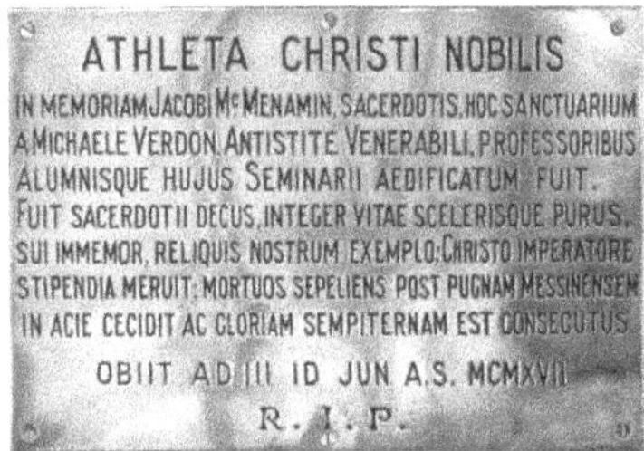

Fennessy, Brian. Holy Cross chapel in Mosgiel. Timaru, New Zealand, 2015

James J. McMenamin was born in Wanganui on 16 August 1874.[38] His father John was an Irish immigrant, who had only arrived in New Zealand four years earlier; soon after he met and married Elizabeth Wrighton.[39] In the 1890s, the McMenamin family moved to Hutt Valley, where James and his brother William established themselves as tailors on Main Hutt Road. Their father, John, had previously worked on the North Island railway systems, until an accident caused him permanent spinal injuries.[40] John's health further deteriorated

38 "Territorial Force - The Reverend James Joseph McMenamin - Chaplain 4th Class, New Zealand Chaplains Department [WWI 6/1215 - Army] [Image 24]," 25 August 1914, Archway, Archives New Zealand, http://goo.gl/A5U9UE

39 B. J. Cullinane, Mission to River Hutt: A History of the Catholic Church in the Hutt Valley and the Parish of Saints Peter & Paul, 1850-2000 (Lower Hutt, N.Z.: Parish of Saints Peter & Paul, 2002), 350.

40 Ibid.

in 1902, when he was sent to the Home for Incurables in Wellington; he remained there until his death in 1925.

The life of a tailor, however, was not a lifelong ambition of James McMenamin. In 1902, he answered God's call and entered the Holy Cross Seminary at Mosgiel.[41] He was 28 years old. On 12 December 1909, James and five others were ordained as priests by Bishop Michael Verdon;[42] they were the first priests ordained in the new chapel at Holy Cross.[43] His first appointment was at Westport, where he stayed until 1912 when he became parish priest at Petone.[44]

All accounts of Father McMenamin describe him as an active and social member of the community. Before joining the priesthood, he and his brother William were fond of cricket; James played first for the Waiwhetu Cricket Club and later the Petone Club.[45] It was his constant activity and presence that allowed him to "rapidly" become "a pillar of the community."[46]

Perhaps it was his endless energy that motivated him to volunteer when war was declared. He was attested for service as early as 25 August 1914,[47] only a few weeks after New Zealand committed herself to fighting for the Empire, and was assigned to the Canterbury Infantry.[48] Given the rank of Chaplain IVth class, Captain McMenamin sailed with the main body of the New Zealand Expeditionary Force

41 Ibid.

42 Peter Joseph Norris, Southernmost Seminary: The story of Holy Cross College, Mosgiel (1900-97), Holy Cross Seminary, Auckland, 1999), 11-15.

43 Cullinane, 350.

44 Ibid, 351.

45 Ibid.

46 Theodore Loretz, "100 Kiwi Stories: Chaplain's Courage Inspired Many," New Zealand Herald, March 19, 2015, accessed July 3, 2015, http://goo.gl/qZ41aN

47 Cullinane, 351.

48 "Territorial Force - The Reverend James Joseph McMenamin [Image 27]."

on 16 October 1914.[49] The fleet arrived in Alexandria on 3 December 1914, where they proceeded to Zeitoun Camp for further training.[50]

On 25 January 1915, reconnaissance showed that Turkish forces were moving towards the Suez Canal; the New Zealand Infantry Brigade - including the Auckland and Canterbury Battalions - were sent to Ismailia, located halfway between the Canal and Port Said.[51] Captain McMenamin accompanied his regiment, managing to hold Mass with whatever was at hand, such as "a doctor's operation table" serving as an altar.[52] The battalion remained near the Canal until 26 February, when it finally returned to Zeitoun Camp outside of Cairo.[53]

Captain McMenamin was among the first New Zealand troops who landed at Anzac Cove on 25 April 1915. Over the next four months, McMenamin saw the worst of the Gallipoli campaign. During the landing itself, more than 200 men from the Canterbury Battalion were declared killed, wounded or missing.[54] In a letter to fellow priest and chaplain, Leo Daly, McMenamin wrote:

> *I have scribbled these few notes hastily on my knees while we are taking a rest. Nearly all the time shells have been bursting all around us and I have been expecting one to drop in my face at any time so I am afraid my notes*

49 Capt. David Ferguson, The History of the Canterbury Regiment, N.Z.E.F. 1914-1919 (Melbourne, N.Z.: Whitcomb and Tombs, Ltd., 1921), NZETC, 9. It is unclear whether or not McMenamin sailed aboard the SS Athenic or the RMS Tahiti. Both steamships sailed from Lyttleton, Christchurch, Canterbury, on 16 October 1914, headed for Egypt and the Dardanelles Campaign.

50 "Territorial Force - The Reverend James Joseph McMenamin [Image 26]."

51 Ferguson, 13.

52 Loretz, "100 Kiwi Stories."

53 Ferguson, 17-18.

54 Ibid, 28.

will sound somewhat jumbled to you ... I have just been interrupted to go and bury two Otago Boys (1RC) ... just been killed by the shrapnel...[55]

He survived the landing at Gallipoli and daily firefights between the Anzacs and Turks along Walker's Ridge; he survived the horrors of the "Daisy Patch," multiple assaults on Sari Bair, as well as the Chunuk Bair offensive. It is little wonder that Captain McMenamin's health weakened to such a point that he was evacuated from the front on 9 September 1915,[56] returning thence to New Zealand for recuperation.[57] According to a letter written by Father Patrick Dore, McMenamin was suffering from influenza in late July, which might have had lingering effects on his constitution.[58]

On 30 October 1915, McMenamin returned home upon the troopship *Willochra*, whereafter he spent his recovery period in Ponsonby Parish.[59] He continued to serve the community, although he was still of frail health; in January 1916 he recounted his experiences at Gallipoli "to a packed congregation at Sacred Heart Church" in Ponsonby Auckland. He remained seated throughout his address.[60]

Ill health did not dissuade McMenamin from returning to service for King and Country. In May 1916, he sailed to England,

55 Cullinane, 351. These ellipses are original to the text.

56 "Territorial Force - The Reverend James Joseph McMenamin - Chaplain 4th Class, New Zealand Chaplains Department [WWI 6/1215 - Army] [Image 29 & 42]," 7 June 1915, Archway, Archives New Zealand, http://goo.gl/jFo2eQ

57 "McMenamin, James Joseph - WWI 6/1215 - Army [Image 3]," 13 August 1921, Archway, Archives New Zealand, http://goo.gl/J55mp1

58 "Fighting on Gallipoli," Evening Post, 4 August 1915, accessed July 4, 2015, http://goo.gl/SNw0B1

59 "Praise for Chaplains," New Zealand Herald, November 1, 1915, accessed July 4, 2015, http://goo.gl/DOsuRv

60 Cullinane, 351.

where he administered the sick, wounded and dying returning from the front lines in France and Belgium.[61] McMenamin was also made Lieutenant-Colonel and "organising chaplain for all the Roman Catholic chaplains" from New Zealand.[62] In January 1917, McMenamin returned to the front, serving with the Canterbury Regiment near Messines.

The *Colonist* published an extract of a letter, dated 8 June 1917, from a young, Petone soldier, who was a patient in an English hospital, describing McMenamin's ministry:

> *Father McMenamin is known as Father Mac. He is right out on his own. When he is not settling draught problems for us he is accompanying embryo Sims Reeves on the piano, and is always looking after the boys, who swear by him. The way the boys borrow an occasional 5s from him is pretty strong. Catholic, Jew or Protestant, it is all the same. There's no creed or colour drawn by Father Mac. Good luck to him.*[63]

In June 1914, the Allied forces undertook operations to capture the town of Messines and Wytschaete Ridge as part of a preliminary phase in the greater Passchendaele Offensive.[64] Beginning on 7 June, the British, Australian and New Zealand forces swept across no-man's land as their artillery bombarded the German lines. It was a successful prelude to the later tragedy of Passchendaele, but it was not without its casualties. More than 600 men were killed or wounded during the three-

61 "McMenamin, James Joseph - WWI 6/1215 - Army [Image 3]."

62 "A Popular Padre," Sun, June 14 1917, accessed July 3, 2015, http://goo.gl/ZHP01H

63 "Personal," Colonist, June 8, 1917, accessed, July 4 2015, http://goo.gl/0U18eY

64 Ferguson, 151.

day Battle of Messines;[65] Chaplain McMenamin was among them. On 9 June, he was officiating the burial of soldiers who fell during the battle when a German shell exploded nearby, killing him instantly.[66] He was 43 years old.

Chaplain Major James J. McMenamin, having been promoted just before his death, was first buried by Father Patrick O'Neill, from the Dunedin Diocese, and then reinterred in a vault under the crucifix at St. Martin's Church, in the Nieppe Communal Cemetery, near Armentieres, France.[67] He was described by his former commanding officer, Colonel H. Stewart, as "a man of the highest character, unsurpassable courage and kindly disposition."[68] At home, a Requiem Mass was held in his honour "at the Basilica in Hill Street," as well as in his own parish in Petone.[69] After McMenamin's death, Chaplain Taylor, an Anglican, wrote of his efforts at Gallipoli in the NZ Tablet:

> *The Dardanelles brought out the revelation of his supreme courage, no place was too hot for him if there was work to do, no task too simple if he could cheer or help someone; he carried water, he helped the wounded to the beach, he even went with the wounded to the transport; he was up night after night just doing good.*[70]

65 Ibid, 165-66.

66 Ibid, 352.

67 "McMenamin, James Joseph - WWI 6/1215 - Army [Image 2]."

68 Cullinane, 352.

69 Ibid.

70 "A Gallant Chaplain," New Zealand Herald, June 18, 1917, accessed July 5, 2015, http://goo.gl/sYDyKI

Fennessy, Brian. Chaplain-Major James L. McMenamin Memorial.

Timaru, New Zealand, 2015

CHAPTER 3

Chaplain-Captain Guy S. Bryan-Brown

KIA, Passchendaele, 4 October 1917

Guy Spencer Bryan-Brown was not born in New Zealand, nor did his family emigrate when he was young. Guy was born 3 July 1885 in Amberley, West Sussex, England to Reverend Willoughby and Mrs. Grace Bryan-Brown.[71] He attended Downing College, Cambridge, where he received his degree (with honours) in Theology in 1907.[72] After another year spent at Ridley Hall, he took his Holy Orders and also received a Teaching Diploma.[73] Immediately after school, he was ordained as a priest by the Bishop of London in 1910,[74] then sent north as a Master and Chaplain at Trinity College, Glenalmond, Perth, Scotland.[75]

It was not until 1913, when Guy (then 28 years old) emigrated to New Zealand to take up the position as chaplain and school master at Christ's College in Christchurch.[76] Guy was exceedingly active, just like his brothers. His life was a

---

71 "Bryan-Brown, Guy Spencer - WWI 41286 - Army [Image 42]," 16 June 1917, Archway, Archives New Zealand, http://goo.gl/YBHvri

72 "The Fallen and Wounded," Press, June 29, 1917, accessed July 1, 2015, http://goo.gl/ZMCs7f

73 "Personal," Auckland Star, April 25, 1913, accessed July 1, 2015, http://goo.gl/Gh0H6v

74 "Christ's College," Press, April 23, 1913, accessed July 1, 2015, http://goo.gl/m84Spf

75 Andrew Renshaw, Wisden on the Great War: The Lives of Cricket's Fallen 1914-1918, (London: Bloomsbury Publishing, 2014), 310.

76 "Christ's College."

series of activities. His obituary described him as "a splendid athlete. He represented Canterbury in the cricket field, and was also prominent in hockey circles."[77] In fact, while at Cambridge, he became Captain of his college Cricket XI, Hockey XL and Tennis Club; he even received the Blue for hockey.[78] He continued his athletics when in New Zealand and soon added military training to his repertoire. One of his colleagues later remarked:

> *To my mind he was ideal as a Schoolmaster. He has left behind him at Glenalmond and in N.Z., and with his friends in every place a most sacred influence. Everybody loved him. Boy after boy can vouch for the help and guidance he gave them, and we who are older owe him more than words can say. One always came away from a talk with him the stronger and better.*[79]

Bryan-Brown became a Captain in the Officer Training Corps in 1913, after arriving at his new home. As of March 1914, he had attested as a Chaplain to the Territorial Force and was involved in the cadet unit at Christ's College.[80] It was remarked by his peers at Christ's College that Bryan-Brown "increasingly felt the need to be at the front."[81] In late 1916, Chaplain Bryan-Brown declined a nomination to be posted

77 "For King and Empire," Sun, October 12, 1917, accessed July 1, 2015, http://goo.gl/4CFz1b

78 Ibid.

79 Tonbridge School and the Great War of 1914-1919, (Tonbridge, N.Z.: Whitefriars Press, Ltd., 1923), 48.

80 "In Black & White," Christ's College Canterbury, Issue 70 (2014, June 17): 8, accessed July 1, 2015, https://goo.gl/mdwALV

81 Anthony Seldon & David Walsh, Public Schools and the Great War: The Generation Lost (Barnsley, South Yorkshire, U.K.: Pen & Sword Military, 2013), 76.

to the Hospital Ship, SS *Maheno*, electing instead to accept a post within the 21st Reinforcements of the New Zealand Expeditionary Force.[82]

Guy attested for Regular Service on 6 January 1917 and set sail for England later that month upon the *Ulimaroa*.[83] Upon arrival in Plymouth, Chaplain Bryan-Brown was attached to the 3rd Battalion Canterbury Regiment, 7 April 1917, arriving in France on 29 May 1917. He was wounded in action on 12 June 1917, just fourteen days after his arrival; he did, however, remain on duty with his unit.[84]

General Haig's Passchendaele Offensive, which began on 31 July 1917, was intended to "turn the Belgian flank of the German Army,"[85] thereby opening access to the Belgian coast and limiting the impact of German submarines. In order to achieve this plan, the Allies conducted a series of 'pushes' along the Belgian front; the Australians were charged with taking Broodseinde Ridge, while the New Zealand Division looked to Gravenstafel Spur.[86] The New Zealanders attacked on 4 October after a heavy barrage of artillery wore down the German front line. The objective and a large number of prisoners were taken, not to mention that the casualties were low. Allied command presumed this represented a weakened enemy and considered the 'push' a success.[87]

More than 1,000 New Zealanders were wounded on 4 October and over 300 lost their lives, including Chaplain-

---

82 The nomination was made by the Primate, The Right Reverend Samuel Nevill.

83 Tonbridge School and the Great War of 1914-1919, 48.

84 "Bryan-Brown, Guy Spencer - WWI 41286 - Army [Image 41]."

85 Frank E. Vandiver, "Field Marshal Sir Douglas Haig and Passchendaele," in Passchendaele in Perspective: The Third Battle of Ypres, ed. Peter H. Liddle (Barnsley, South Yorkshire, U.K.: Pen & Sword Military, 2013), 39.

86 Ferguson, 183-204.

87 Ibid, 190.

Major Bryan-Brown.[88] On that day, like so many before it, the Chaplain was at work at an advanced dressing station, tending to the wounded as they returned from the front line. His colleague, Chaplain Francis Bartley, recalled that day, saying, "'Brown worked like ten men all day attending the wounded. Our pillbox was shelled repeatedly but, in spite of all, Brown was constantly outside helping the men lying on stretchers for whom there was no room inside.'"[89] Bartley continued,

> 'About 4pm we proposed to block up the 'windows', the middle one of which had been blown in at about 9.30am. I was working on this larger opening when Brown, having finished the inside of his two smaller ones, went outside to brick them up from the outside. At once three shells struck the building and I saw him stagger and fall. I rushed out to him, pronouncing the words of the Absolution, as I ran, but he was dead when I reached him. He had been hit at the back of the left thigh, which had been badly torn, but I think that death was due to shock. The calmness on his face showed that all was painless. God rest his gallant soul ....[90]

Bartley buried his comrade near their pillbox, located by Otto Farm. Bryan-Brown was 32 years old when he died.

The continuation of the Passchendaele Offensive resulted in further shelling of the Allied lines, which sadly destroyed

88 Ibid, 204.

89 J. Bryant Haigh, Men of Faith and Courage: The Official history of the Royal New Zealand Chaplains Department (Auckland, N.Z.: Word Publishers, 1983), 69.

90 Haigh, 69.

Bryan-Brown's grave.[91] His name and memory are recorded at the Tyne Cot Memorial, near Passchendaele. Christ's College honoured him also, both with a commemorative fireplace and hearth in the library of Jacob's House, and also in a commemorative window in the south transept of the chapel.[92] One of his colleagues at Christ's College, a Staff Captain, and officer of N.Z. Pioneers, wrote of his fallen friend,

> *The doctors who were with him say that he rendered invaluable assistance during the day in bringing in and dressing the wounded, and I am sure from what I know of him that he never spared himself or thought for one moment of the risk he was running, so long as he could help those who were in need. ... We all loved him for his cheery, honest, open way, and though his time at the College was short, his influence will be with us long.*[93]

91 Ibid.

92 "About Jacobs House," Christ College Canterbury, accessed July 1, 2015, http://christscollege.com/about-college/houses/jacobs/about.

93 Tonbridge School and the Great War of 1914-1919, 48.

CHAPTER 4

Chaplain-Captain Alexander Allen

KIA, Somme, 8 May 1918

Annie Allen gave birth to her only child, Alexander, on 1 January 1884 in Timaru.[94] Alexander would go on to attend school at the Methodist Theological College, as well as at Auckland University College, participating in the University Hockey Club and Debating Society.[95] In 1913, he played on the senior squad for the Te Rangi; he joined them again in 1915 when the Te Rangi found themselves a few players short in a match against St. Mary's.[96] In early 1914, Alexander became a fully accredited Methodist minister and continued working locally in Timaru.[97]

On 4 April 1914 in Hastings, Rev. Allen married Eva Sandford, daughter of the late Mr. E. Sandford, a former member of Parliament for Christchurch City.[98] Thereafter, the couple moved to Waikouaiti. A farewell service was given for the reverend at the Bank Street Methodist Church, where he had been stationed for nearly two years; the audience was

94 "Wedding," Timaru Herald, April 9, 1914, accessed July 4, 2015, http://goo.gl/3LeX2s

95 "New Zealand and World War One," Auckland Weekly News - Personnel Paragraphs, May 1918, accessed July 3, 2015, http://goo.gl/fce3zh

96 "Hockey," Timaru Herald, May 22, 1915, accessed July 4, 2015, http://goo.gl/mEYCQw

97 "Personal Items," Timaru Herald, February 25, 1914, accessed, July 4, 2015, http://goo.gl/P45fg9

98 "New Zealand and World War One."

said to be "overflowing" with well-wishers.[99] Mr. and Mrs. Allen then lived in Waikouaiti for another two years where Reverend Allen became active in supporting the war effort. The Otago Daily Times recorded more than one occasion when Allen and his parishioners raised money for the Belgian Relief Fund.[100]

The Allens moved to Caversham in early 1916 and were warmly welcomed by the new congregation. Reverend Allen was said to have come "with the highest credentials for the spiritual welfare of the church and for the keen interest in all that pertains to the youth of the church."[101] Once again, they became active participants in the community. More than one newspaper article recalled the reverend's organisation of a local social or concert. One such concert occurred at the Abbotsford Methodist Church in order to raise funds for the congregation; Rev. Allen sang several duets "with marked effect."[102] His popularity among the many communities wherein he ministered was well recorded in the contemporary, local papers, but it was not to last. Like many of his compatriots, Allen left his family and friends behind to fight for King and Empire.

The records indicate that Chaplain-Captain A. Allen embarked on 14 March 1917 upon the RMS *Ruapehu* steamship and arrived in Plymouth, England on 21 May

---

99 "Rev. A. Allen," Timaru Herald, 30 March 1914, accessed July 4, 2015, http://goo.gl/l6e8nc

100 "Belgian Relief Fund," Otago Daily Times, June 15, 1915, accessed July 5, 2015, http://goo.gl/NnEx2C; "The Otago Patriotic Fund," Otago Daily Times, September 2, 1915, accessed July 5, 2015, http://goo.gl/YlpVRO

101 "Caversham Methodist Church," Otago Daily Times, April 14, 1916, accessed July 5, 2015, http://goo.gl/FGyevZ

102 "Abbotsford Methodist Church," Otago Daily Times, October 13, 1916, accessed July 4, 2015, http://goo.gl/r74F2F

1917.[103] It was during his voyage to England that his mother, Annie, passed away; condolences were sent by the Caversham Methodist Church back home.[104] When in England, he was assigned to the No. 2 New Zealand General Hospital, located at Walton-on-Thames, Surrey.[105] As of 1915, the hospital officially became the New Zealand War Contingent Hospital for the immediate needs of the wounded returning from the Gallipoli Campaign.[106] Over time, the hospital expanded to house more than 1,500 patients; an estimated 27,000 New Zealanders were tended during the war.[107] Chaplain Allen was among those who saw to the convalescent and spiritual needs of the men returning from the front.

On 15 September, Chaplain Allen, attached to the 23rd Reinforcements, arrived in France. Thereafter he joined the 4th Battalion, 3rd New Zealand Rifle Brigade at Doulieu, a French town located roughly 15 kilometres west of Armentieres.[108] Here the 4th recuperated after their efforts in the Warneton Sector, not far from Messines, where the weather was "atrocious" and the "artillery and aerial activity were ... unusually intense."[109] Allen administered to the wounded at the Regimental Aid Post; he took on the casualties from the Third Battle of Ypres, as well as those who would arrive after the Germans launched their final offensive in 1918.

103 "Alexander Allen," Auckland War Memorial Museum, accessed July 4, 2015, http://goo.gl/POQCYs

104 "General News," Otago Daily Times, April 7, 1917, accessed July 4, 2015, http://goo.gl/Nj6IYi

105 "Allen, Alexander - WWI 48144 - Army [Image 4]," June 30, 1917, Archway, Archives New Zealand, http://goo.gl/WXFxKf

106 Lt. H. T. B. Drew, ed. The War Effort of New Zealand (Auckland, N.Z.: Whitcombe and Tombs, Ltd., 1923), NZETC, 117.

107 Ibid, 119.

108 Lieut.-Col. W. S. Austin, The Official History of the New Zealand Rifle Brigade (Wellington, N.Z.: L. T. Watkins Ltd., 1924), NZETC, 222.

109 Ibid, 225. The Warneton Sector or Line is located two miles southeast of Messines.

In 1918, the Germans put all their effort into breaking through the Allied lines along the Western Front. Reinforcements had recently arrived from the dismantled Eastern Front, which provided them with the manpower required to give one last push against the weakened Allied armies.[110] Between March and April 1918, the Germans bombarded the Allied artillery, headquarters and communications lines with heavy shellfire. Over 3,200 New Zealanders were killed or wounded in this single month of fighting.[111] In the aftermath of the bombardment and skirmishes, Chaplain-Captain Alexander Allen, while tending to the wounded in the Regimental Aid Post, was killed by a random enemy shell.

> *Hostile shelling throughout the month (i.e. May) was on the whole below normal, the enemy confining himself in the main to periodical shell-storms. On the 8th, the 4th Battalion aid-post near the Sugar Factory, was wrecked by a heavy shell, both the medical officer, Capt. A. M. Tolhurst, and the chaplain, the Revd. A. Allen, being killed.*[112]

Allen was 34 years old when he died in France, leaving behind his wife Eva and a son born after he had sailed to England. His remains were buried in Doullens Communal Cemetery Extension No. 2, located in northern France.[113] In June 1918,

110 Randal Gray, Kaiserchlacht 1918 - The Final German Offensive, (University Park, IL: Osprey Publishing, Ltd., 2002), 29.

111 "First World War Casualties by Month," Ministry for Culture and Heritage, last updated November 4, 2014, accessed June 30, 2015, http://goo.gl/EIn6Ew

112 Lieut.-Col. W. S. Austin, 320.

113 "Allen, The Rev. Alexander," Commonwealth War Graves Commission, accessed July 4, 2015, http://goo.gl/fRd0kl

the Waikouaiti Methodist Church, where he had ministered between 1914-1916, held a memorial service in his honour. There the Reverend W. B. Pickering "spoke of Mr. Allen's striking personality, of his great abilities as a singer, which made him popular with all; [and] of his Christian courage and devotion to the course of his Master."[114] He was posthumously awarded the British War Medal in September 1921 and then the Victory Medal in July 1922; both of these medals, along with a scroll and plaque, were sent to his widow, care of Messrs Field & Royds, 200 Cashel Street, Christchurch.[115] A plaque in his memory now exists in the Caversham Methodist Church, Dunedin.[116]

114 "Memorial Services," Otago Daily Times, June 7, 1918, accessed July 5, 2015, http://goo.gl/HN6MBP

115 "Allen, Alexander - WWI 48144 - Army [Image 4]."

116 "Tale of a Methodist Minister," Fairfax Media Digital Edition, November 19, 2014, accessed July 5, 2015.

CHAPTER 5

Chaplain-Captain Patrick Dore

Wounded, Gallipoli, 15 July 1918

Died, Auckland, NZ, 22 August 1918

Image from 1987.1647 National Army Museum, NZ

It is often difficult to piece together the stories of men from 100 years ago, especially if national or local records are incomplete. Future chaplain Patrick Dore emigrated to New Zealand in 1910 from Ireland. Recently ordained, he took up a post as curate at St. Patrick's Church, Palmerston North, upon arrival and remained there for a year before transferring to Kaikoura parish (1912)[117] and then to Foxton (1913).[118] Before coming to New Zealand, sources provide little information on Dore's past. It is noted in several newspaper articles and on his service records that he was born 4 February 1886 in Co. Limerick, Ireland; an "M. Dore" is cited as his father who remained in Ireland.[119] Beyond this basic information, Dore's early years remain a mystery.

Accounts of his disposition and activities are more pronounced during his time in New Zealand. His connection with the parishioners he served is most notable. When leaving Palmerston North, for example, he was gifted "with an umbrella and rug from the ladies, and a cigar case, suitably inscribed, from the male members of the church."[120] The official history of the *Auckland Mounted Rifles*, chapter XIII, commented,

> Few men of the N.Z.E.F. had the wide popularity of Father Dore. Denominational distinctions carried little weight in the Regiment, especially in those days of grim realities, and least of all did they weigh with Father Dore. He was the friend and counsellor of everyone. Wherever he went he took cheer, and raised a laugh when a laugh was badly

117 "Local and General," Evening Post, February 4, 1911, accessed July 5, 2015, http://goo.gl/3e3gkC; "Personal Items," Press, February 28, 1912, accessed July 5, 2015, http://goo.gl/2M6qaN

118 "Personal," Manawatu Standard, February 1, 1913, accessed July 5, 2015, http://goo.gl/1xn1sO

119 "Patrick Dore," Auckland War Memorial Museum, accessed July 4, 2015, http://www.aucklandmuseum.com/war-memorial/online-cenotaph/record/C32143.

120 "Personal Items," Press, 28 February 28, 1912, accessed July 5, 2015, http://goo.gl/J2sOGG

needed. During the long days of defensive war he made it his business to visit parties in the worst and most dangerous saps, and his magnetic personality always helped to ease the load for over-burdened men. His presence was a better tonic than any the doctor could give, and he will always be kept in affectionate remembrance by Gallipoli veterans.[121]

When War was declared, Dore, like McMenamin, immediately offered his services as a Catholic chaplain to the Expeditionary Force. He enlisted in early August 1914 and was posted as Chaplain IV class to the Auckland Mounted Rifles (AMRs).[122] The AMRs, all three squadrons of which were filled "within a few days of the call for volunteers,"[123] trained at Epsom Camp until orders for embarkation arrived in late September.[124] The Rifles, split between the HMNZ *Waimana* and HMNZ *Star of India*, were only at sea for 24 hours before turning back towards Auckland Harbour; two German cruisers had been seen in the Southern Pacific.[125] The threat forced the AMRs to endure further training in Otahuhu and Taka-puna until October.

The AMRs, Dore among them, finally set off for Egypt on 16 October 1914, arriving in Alexandria aboard the *Star of India* on 3 December 1914.[126] They encamped in Zeitoun outside of Cairo with their compatriots, enjoying the same rigorous training and moments of tourism as their Australian counterparts. The AMRs had a regimental strength of 26

121 Sergt. C. G. Nicol, The Story of Two Campaigns: Official War History of the Auckland Mounted Rifles Regiment, 1914-1919 (Auckland, N.Z.: Wilson & Horton, 1921), 84.

122 "Dore, Patrick - WWI 13/655 - Army [Image 4]," Auckland War Memorial Museum, accessed July 5, 2015, http://goo.gl/qBqlcl

123 Sergt. C. G. Nicol, 3.

124 Ibid.

125 Ibid, 8-9.

126 "Dore, Patrick - WWI 13/655 - Army [Image 3]."

officers and 482 men of other ranks, including Chaplain Dore; the regiment's 71 horses would not land on the Gallipoli Peninsula. The regiment sailed on the HMT *Grentully Castle* with the Australian Light Horse on May 9, landing at Anzac Cove on 12 May. The arrival of the mounted brigades, like Dore's AMRs and Chaplain-Major Grant's Wellington MRs (Chapter 1), were used to fill gaps in the infantry's lines, caused by two weeks of constant fighting.[127]

On 13 May, the AMRs were moved into position on Walker's Ridge. Here they dug in and felt the weight of Turkish guns from the higher ground. An attack was launched late on the 18th by the Turks, whose artillery bombarded the New Zealand troops, killing 22 and wounding another 27.[128] During the next two months, the AMRs suffered shelling and sniper shots while moving in and out of position on Walker's Ridge. They received reinforcements on 30 June to restore their dwindling numbers. All the while, Dore tended the wounded alongside the Medical Corps. In a letter to Archbishop O'Shea, dated 6 May, Dore wrote,

> *Our poor boys ... have lost quite a large number of officers and men ... Father Finn, of the Dublin Fusiliers, was hit four times in the chest while on the boat going from the ship to the beach. ... An hour after arriving on land he was struck by another bullet in the head. He died within an hour. ... Two days after landing the Dublins and Munsters were able to muster only a company between them. ... the work*

127 Patrick Gariepy, Gardens of Hell: Battles of the Gallipoli Campaign (Nebraska: University of Nebraska Press, 2014), 117-18.

128 Sergt. C. G. Nicol, 42-43.

> *attending to the wounded is growing exceedingly heavy. ... fresh cases come in every day, and more hospitals are being opened, which makes a lot of work for one priest.*[129]

Between 21 and 28 August, the Allies made another assault on the Turks with the objective of taking control of Hill 60. It was in this conflict, on 28 August, that Chaplain-Major Grant was shot in an enemy trench while tending to the wounded. Chaplain-Captain Dore fell during the same offensive, seeing to similar needs of his wounded brethren. The official history of the AMRs recounts Dore's last moments with them as ones of bravery and courage:

> *The beloved padre had gone with Captain Jory, the new medical officer of the Regiment, and four stretcher-bearers, to assist with the wounded in Aghyl Dere—wounded of other regiments of course. He was struck in the region of the spine, and would speedily have succumbed if he had been left at any of the dressing stations, but through the devotion of Trooper Foley and others of the stretcher-bearers, he was conveyed to the beach in spite of the system which required the wounded to go from one party to another.*[130]

Chaplain-Captain Dore was swiftly taken to Devonport, England, where medical personnel noted that he had partial paralysis in his right leg below the knee.[131] He was repatriated to

129 "Dying Chaplain's Heroism," New Zealand Herald, June 23, 1915, accessed July 5, 2015, http://goo.gl/DkpKpa

130 Sergt. C. G. Nicol, 83-84.

131 "Territorial Force - The Reverend Father Patrick Dore, M.C. - Chaplain -Captain, New Zealand Chaplains Department [WWI 12/655 - Army [Images 53-54]," Auckland War Memorial Museum, accessed July 5, 2015, http://goo.gl/2ApvSC

New Zealand on the troopship SS *Willochra* in late 1916; he had not fully recovered from his wounds.[132] He appeared at various gatherings in Palmerston,[133] Wellington[134] and Auckland, the latter being a Requiem Mass for the late Father McMenamin.[135] Dore's discomfort, however, did not cease. The wound had become infected, forcing him to return to Auckland for surgery after a quick visit to his old parish in Foxton. Dore died from surgical complications at Mater Misericordiae Hospital on 15 July 1918.[136] He was 32 years old.

Father Dore was awarded the Military Cross in January 1916 for his actions in Gallipoli, while still in the Devonport military hospital. It was not until after his death that he would receive the Star British War Medal and Victory Medal.[137] Archbishop Redwood led a Requiem Mass for the late Dore, but it is perhaps his surviving comrades-in-arms that spoke most poignantly of their friend: "His unfailing cheerfulness and his rich Irish humour were a constant source of inspiration to us. He was in ever way a 'big' man .... This regiment will remember him for the things he need not have done."[138] Dore was buried on 17 July 1918 in his own parish of Foxton.[139]

---

132 "Personal," Manawatu Times, September 29, 1916, accessed July 5, 2015, http://goo.gl/OOkRzk

133 "Palmerston Doings," Free Lance, August 4, 1916, accessed July 5, 2015, http://goo.gl/IrGJU6

134 "Memorial Service at Boullcott-Street," Evening Post, April 25, 1917, accessed July 6, 2015, http://goo.gl/CP1XxU

135 "In Memory of the Fallen," New Zealand Herald, June 21, 1917, accessed July 6, 2015, http://goo.gl/oplDEQ

136 "The Late Father Dore," Auckland Star, July 16, 1918, accessed July 6, 2015, http://goo.gl/NYjaio

137 "Dore, Patrick - WWI 13/655 - Army [Image 1]."

138 "Death of Father Dore," New Zealand Herald, July 16, 1918, accessed July 6, 2015, http://goo.gl/zvteoR

139 "Military Funeral," Manawatu Times, July 18, 1918, accessed July 6, 2015, http://goo.gl/KGw3jk

Image from 1987.1647 National Army Museum, NZ

Fennesy, Brian. Chaplain-Captain Patrick Dore. Timaru, New Zealand, 2015

CHAPTER 6

Chaplain-Captain Cecil A. Mallett

Died in a Fire, Étaples, France, 30 September 1918

The life of Cecil Alfred Mallet presents a challenge to chronicle. His military records, written in his own hand, indicate that he was born 27 November 1880 in England; the *Anglican Clergy Directory* (ACD) lists his birthplace as Marylebone.[140] He was the eldest child to Alfred and Emma Mallett of Crayford, Kent.[141] Some sources indicate that the Mallett family traveled to New Zealand together shortly after 1900. Cecil Mallett supposedly worked odd jobs to raise funds for a return to England, sailing upon the *Gothic* in July 1907, aged 27.[142] The ACD, however, places Cecil in England until 1912.[143] All sources agree that he attended the College of St. Augustine in Canterbury between 1910-1912, was curate in Aylesford and Dartford parishes and, after obtaining his Licentiae of Theology (L. Th.), sailed for New Zealand.[144]

140 "Anglican Clergy Directory - Macartney to Mutu." KinderLibrary, accessed July 6, 2015, http://archive.is/YtzKA.

141 Ibid.

142 "Personal," Taranaki Herald, July 9, 1907, accessed July 5, 2015, http://goo.gl/kiv74d. Taranaki Daily News, 10 July 1907 (says Mallett was scheduled to return to England on 18 July. Moreover, the Taranaki Daily News, 16 January 1914, references Mallett having a "commercial position" in New Plymouth before going to England for ministerial education. See also, Hawera & Normanby Star, 9 October 1918. The ACD, however, lists him as an "insurance clerk residing with the family [in] Hampstead[,] London", then provides other positions he held during that time, including: a farm hand, groom's labourer, and commercial traveller.

143 "Anglican Clergy Directory - Macartney to Mutu."

144 "Personal," Colonist, October 11, 1918, accessed July 6, 2015, http://goo.gl/dLp-tUh

In December 1912, Mallett arrived in New Zealand upon the *Ruapehu.*[145] He was posted as the Anglican Home Missioner at Ohura, located near Taranaki in January 1913,[146] before being charged with the care of Morrinsville and Matamata districts two years later.[147] It was at this final post that he met his future wife, May Parkinson; the couple was married in November 1914.[148] The couple appeared several times in local newspapers, playing lawn tennis[149] and participating in choirs[150] within the community.

Rev. Mallet was appointed to the military's Chaplain's Department as early as 27 April 1915,[151] but was not called to active duty until 1917. Upon the death of Chaplain-Captain Bryan-Brown on 4 October 1917, Rev. C. A. Mallett was nominated to take his place by the Bishop of Wellington.[152] He was forced to buy an officer's uniform for £10, as one would not be provided to him.[153] Chaplain IVth Class Mallett reported for duty at Trentham Camp, 15 November 1917, and then sailed with the 32nd Reinforcements New Zealand Infantry from Wellington, on 21 November 1917.[154]

145 "Shipping," Evening Post, 3 December 3, 1912, accessed July 6, 2015, http://goo.gl/eSQ56D

146 "Personal," Manawatu Standard, January 14, 1913, accessed July 6, 2015, http://goo.gl/pPazbb

147 "Country News," New Zealand Herald, February 1, 1915, accessed July 6, 2015, http://goo.gl/O40qwK

148 Andrew Stone, "100 Kiwi Stories: Men of the Cloth Not Spared from Conflict while Doing Their Duty," New Zealand Herald, January 8, 2915, http://goo.gl/2HkAqm

149 "Country News," New Zealand Herald, February 3, 1917, accessed July 6, 2015, http://goo.gl/JKtncw

150 "Waikato Archdeaconry," Waikato Times, September 8, 1916, accessed July 6, 2015, http://goo.gl/nU8eOf

151 "Mallett, Cecil Alfred - WWI 70779 - Army [Image 4]," Auckland War Memorial Museum, accessed July 5, 2015, http://goo.gl/0bF0o1

152 "Mallett, Cecil Alfred - WWI 70779 - Army [Original Paper Personnel File] [Image 27]," Auckland War Memorial Museum, accessed July 5, 2015, http://goo.gl/z16z4z

153 Ibid, Image 29.

154 Ibid, Image 44.

They arrived in Liverpool, England on 8 January 1918, from which Mallett travelled to Brocton, Staffordshire where he made camp with his fellow New Zealanders.[155] Mallett stayed at Brocton until June 1918, where he would have participated in the drills and provided religious services for the soldiers. Among his New Zealand compatriots, he tended to the sick and wounded, offering spiritual comfort and solace to young men thousands of miles from home. It was noted that he and fellow chaplain, Rev. W. Batte, were "indefatigable in looking after the welfare and general entertainment of the Troops."[156]

On 12 June 1918, Mrs. May Mallett gave birth to a daughter, but when her husband received word is unknown.[157] He sailed for France four days later.[158] He was stationed at the New Zealand Base in Étaples, France.

> *The camp was a training base, a depot for supplies, a detention centre for prisoners, and a centre for the treatment of the sick and wounded, with almost twenty general hospitals. At its peak, the camp housed over 100,000 people; altogether, its hospitals could treat 22,000 patients.*[159]

Here Chaplain Mallett helped tend to the wounded returning from the front lines. In August, Étaples experienced yet another air raid, killing two officers.[160] The Chaplain would

155 Ibid.

156 Ibid, Image 7.

157 "Births," New Zealand Herald, June 12, 1918, accessed July 6, 2015, http://goo.gl/8tGjT6

158 "Mallett, Cecil Alfred - WWI 70779 - Army [Original Paper Personnel File] [Image 44]."

159 "Étaples," Through These Lines, June 24, 2011, last modified April 13, 2014, http://goo.gl/52VL9u

160 "August 1st - 31st 1918," Crown Copyright: The National Archives WO95/3991, accessed July 5, 2015, http://www.scarletfinders.co.uk/97.html.

have experienced the over-crowding, sickness and general danger of German attack while the camp, even if he never saw the front line. His death in September, however, was wholly unexpected.

The military records provide a remarkable amount of detail regarding his accidental death. In the early hours of 30 September 1918, fire broke out around the camp, its causes unknown. The dental hut was the only building fully consumed and destroyed, along with its only occupant who bunked there. The official report reads:

> *As soon as possible,* [a] *search was made among the debris & a skeleton was found about 2 yards from the door on the western side. There was nothing by which the skeleton could be identified .... Search was made at once - all over the camp but no trace was found of the chaplain & he has not since been seen or heard of* [since] ....[161]

The newspapers and military reports all stated that Chaplain-Captain Mallet "accidentally burned to death."[162] A court of enquiry found no cause of the fire or why he was unable to escape the dental hut. He was 37 years old. Cecil was survived by two brothers, Capt. H. Mallett, a Military Cross recipient, and Priv. E Mallett, a Military Medal recipient; both of his brothers had been wounded "during the recent fighting."[163]

161 "Mallett, Cecil Alfred - WWI 70779 - Army [Image 2]."

162 "Roll of Honour," New Zealand Herald, October 8, 1918, accessed July 5, 2015, http://goo.gl/EsQeiR

163 "Personal," Colonist, October 11, 1918, accessed July 7, 2015, http://goo.gl/AHFFlt. Although it is not specified, it is most likely that his brothers were fighting along the western front.

Cecil A. Mallett was buried at the Étaples Military Cemetery, France.[164] He was posthumously awarded the British War and Victory Medals (18 December 1923), along with a memorial scroll (9 July 1921) and plaque (20 March 1922).[165] These items were all sent to his widow, who had remarried the Reverend E. H. Gallop,[166] former vicar of Taumarunai, in 1920.[167] After his death, a plaque was placed in St. Matthew's Anglican Church at Morrinsville in his honour.[168]

164 "Cecil Alfred Mallett," Auckland War Memorial Museum, accessed July 8, 2015, http://www.aucklandmuseum.com/war-memorial/online-cenotaph/record/C10262.

165 "Mallett, Cecil Alfred - WWI 70779 - Army [Image 3]."

166 "Higher Education," Hawera & Normanby Star, April 27, 1916, accessed July 5, 2015, http://goo.gl/JPA9cV. It is interesting to note that Rev. Gallop was posted in Taumarunui the same year as the late Rev. Mallett (Auckland Star, 17 February 1913). In 1916, Gallop was transferred back to England, where he became vicar of St. John's, Walham Green.

167 "Personal," Feilding Star, January 18, 1919, accessed July 5, 2015, http://goo.gl/LPw8Q9. An article in the Fielding Star, published in 1919, explained that Mrs. Mallett wished to go to England, "at her own expense," in order to be closer to her husband while he was in France; the authorities would not allow it. It is unclear when she did move to England and reunite with Rev. Gallop.

168 Stone, "100 Kiwi Stories."

CHAPTER 7

Chaplain-Captain Frederick "Francis" Rands

Died of Influenza, Cologne, Germany, 4 February 1919

If some biographies are difficult to piece together from too little information, Frederick Rands' overwhelms from too much evidence. The fifth child of seven children, Frederick Rands was born on 20 March 1883 in Methven, Canterbury. His father Henry had emigrated from Yorkshire, England in 1875 aboard the *Waitangi*.[169] By 1905, he was working with Trinity Methodist Church and "had been most successful in his ministry, endearing himself to everybody who knew him."[170] According to the Auckland University College Roll of Honour, Francis attended school between 1906-1907,[171] although he was a "non-matriculated student."[172]

Eventually Rev. Rands moved to St. Kilda outside Dunedin, where he took on the chair of their Sunday school.[173] From there he ministered in Levin and Wellington South, before moving on to Kaponga in 1912 and, finally, Marton in 1915.[174] While

169 Henry Rands, Autobiography of Henry Rands (Auckland, N.Z.: M. B. Rands,1985), 1-2, 4.

170 "The Methodist Church," Otago Daily Times, September 28, 1905, accessed July 3, 2015, http://goo.gl/FtciIg

171 Jo Birks, "Frederick Rands," First World War Centenary, 2014-2018, accessed July 3, 2015, http://goo.gl/e2DLpI

172 Ibid.

173 "Methodist Church," Otago Daily Times, September 29, 1908, accessed July 6, 2015, http://goo.gl/IIVEAy

174 "Provincial Centres," Dominion, April 20, 1910, accessed July 6, 2015, http://goo.gl/7Tn9sz; "Kaponga," Hawera & Normanby Star, March 15, 1912, accessed July 6, 2015, http://goo.gl/Jzw99W

in Kaponga he married his wife, Dorothy Clark, daughter of the Rev. J. R. Clark of Karori,[175] and had a son, Maxwell, in September 1914.[176] Together, Mr. and Mrs. Rands became active members of the Methodist community, taking part in all aspects of the reverend's vocation.[177]

When not attending religious conferences or ministering to his flock, Francis Rands was feeding his indefatigable athleticism. His name appears multiple times in contemporary newspapers regarding his prowess at tennis[178] or cricket; he was one of several vice-presidents of the St. Kilda Cricket Club.[179] He was even requested to compete as one of Canterbury's athletes in the New Zealand Amateur Athletics Championships to be held 13 March 1915; he was currently posted in Christchurch.[180] Permission was granted and he competed in the long jump.[181] He was also president of Kaponga's hockey club, a sport he had a long history of playing.[182] Rands' keen interest in sports created a deeper connection between himself and his parishioners. There is even a story that he "won over a new church-goer … by

175 "Personal," Manawatu Standard, March 23, 1912, accessed July 6, 2015, http://goo.gl/50OIsX.

176 "Territorial Force - The Reverend Frederick Rands - Chaplain 4th Class, New Zealand Chaplains Department [WWI 42884 - Army] [File 53]," Auckland War Memorial Museum, accessed July 5, 2015, http://goo.gl/HWJmOy

177 "Church Services," Hawera & Normanby Star, January 3, 1913, accessed July 4, 2015, http://goo.gl/dcG7Td; "Marton's New Methodist Minister," Wanganui Chronicle, May 8, 1915, accessed July 7, 2015, http://goo.gl/83lSmr

178 "Athletic Sports," Dominion, December 13, 1910; "Tennis," Horowhenua Chronicle, April 3, 1911; "Tennis," Hawera and Normanby Star, February 16, 1915; "Marton's New Methodist Minister," Wanganui Chronicle, April 12, 1915.

179 "St. Kilda Cricket Club," Otago Witness, 9 September 9, 1908, accessed July 6, 2015, http://goo.gl/Qjd2yg

180 "Athletic Sports," Dominion, 3 March 1915, accessed July 7, 2015, http://goo.gl/ePZVwl

181 "N.Z.A.A.A.," Sun, March 4, 1915, accessed July 6, 2015, http://goo.gl/vDGgP0

182 "Hockey," New Zealand Herald, June 8, 1907, accessed July 6, 2015, http://goo.gl/nWDgrD; "Hockey," Evening Post, May 6, 1911, accessed July 6, 2015, http://goo.gl/G2vLB2

successfully completing a challenge to chop a pile of wood within a certain time."[183]

In January 1916, Rev. F. Rands was made Chaplain Class Four to the New Zealand Expeditionary Forces.[184] He was nominated to replace Chaplain A. Seamer, who had recently been called to the front with the 23rd Reinforcements, at Trentham camp.[185] Rands was described as "manly, athletic, and suitable … for the work" he would be doing at the camp's Methodist Institute.[186] His position within the training camp did not, however, restrict his activities among former parishes. On 4 August 1917, he travelled by express to be a part of St. Kilda Church's war anniversary services.[187] In November, he attended the Wellington Methodist Synod where he "gave a most interesting address on the work of the chaplains among the soldiers."[188]

Less than a month after his daughter was born,[189] Chaplain-Captain Rands boarded the SS *Willochra* with the 36th Reinforcements, headed for Egypt.[190] Rands was well-received by the men during their journey north, according to the company's magazine, Port Light.

183 Maxwell Rands, Memoirs of a Minor Chemist (Auckland, N.Z.: 1993), 1, 3, quoted in "Frederick Rands," First World War Centenary, accessed July 7, 2015, http://goo.gl/w7AR-LW

184 "Military Appointments," Auckland Star, February 1, 1916, accessed July 7, 2015, http://paperspast.natlib.govt.nz/cgi-

185 "Territorial Force - The Reverend Frederick Rands [File 41]."

186 Ibid. "Personal," Feilding Star, February 6, 1917, accessed July 7, 2015, http://goo.gl/nUhbIu

187 "War Anniversary Services," Otago Daily Times, August 4, 1917, accessed July 7, 2015, http://goo.gl/tXqRQX

188 "Methodism," Evening Post, November 21, 1917, accessed July 7, 2015, http://goo.gl/N8tXY2

189 "Territorial Force - The Reverend Frederick Rands [File 53]."

190 "Rands, Frederick - WWI 42884 - Army [Image 2]," Auckland War Memorial Museum, accessed July 7, 2015, http://goo.gl/jrhGEj

> The Padre and the Reps. went amongst the men and obtained a list of everything required by them. The result was a varied and large collection of all manner of goods, which were faithfully delivered to the grateful men.
>
> The spiritual welfare of the men has been kept steadily in view. ... Soon we shall be passing to sterner things, but the knowledge that the Y.M.C.A. is with us makes cheerful thinking. "May the Y.M.C.A. continue in its good work" is the earnest prayer of the soldiers of the 36th Reinforcement.[191]

At the end of May 1918, the 36th disembarked and settled into camp near Suez.[192] A few days later the 36th set out for Alexandria, where they boarded the *Ormonde* and sailed to England.[193] Chaplain Rands, however, was not among them. According to his medical records, he remained in Egypt until September due to sickness.[194] Rands was thereafter attached to an Entrenching Group at the end of September[195] and then, finally, joined the 1st Battalion Auckland Regiment in France.[196]

Between mid-September and November 1918, a second wave of influenza spread across Europe. Before it ended, "tens of millions" had died; casualties among medical personnel

191 The Port Light: N.Z.E.F. 36th Reinfs. : H.M.N.Z.T. Willochra, at Sea, (Auckland, N.Z.: Abel Dykes, Ltd., 1918?), 33.

192 Ibid, 9.

193 Ibid, 9-10.

194 "Territorial Force - The Reverend Frederick Rands [File 50]." On the second page of Rands' history sheet, his ailment is listed as diarrhoea; "Rands, Frederick - WWI 42884 - Army [Image 2]."

195 "Territorial Force - The Reverend Frederick Rands [File 50]."

196 "On Service," Evening Post, January 16, 1919, accessed July 7, 2015, http://goo.gl/NtZ2En; "Territorial Force - The Reverend Frederick Rands [File 50]."

were particularly high.[197] The disease spread quickly and took a heavy toll on the armies, which were now at peace. Poor sanitary conditions, overcrowding and general poor health made the soldiers - and civilians - easy targets. One such victim was Chaplain Rands, who fell ill with the disease and died, 14 February 1919, at a casualty clearing station in Cologne, Germany.[198] He was 35 years old.

His obituary, appearing on 21 February 1919, described him as having a "genial disposition" and as being "widely respected, particularly among the men in camps in New Zealand, with whom his influence for good was widespread."[199] He was posthumously awarded the British War and Victory Medals; a plaque and scroll were also delivered to his widow in 1921.[200] During a Methodist Church conference in late February 1919, a conference of which he was so often a member, the congregation recalled Reverend Rands with these fond words:

> *He was possessed of strong mental, social and spiritual qualities, and he has left fragrant memories in the various parts of New Zealand, wherein he exercised his ministry.*[201]

He was buried in the Cologne Southern Cemetery in Germany.[202]

197 P. C. Wever and L. van Bergen, "Death from 1918 pandemic influenza during the First World War: A Perspective from Personal and Anecdotal Evidence," Influenza and Other Respiratory Viruses 8 (2014), accessed July 7, 2015, doi: 10.1111/irv.12267.

198 "Rands, Frederick - WWI 42884 - Army [Image 2]."

199 "Obituary," Otago Daily Times, February 21, 1919, accessed July 7, 2015, goo.gl/NtZ2En

200 "Rands, Frederick - WWI 42884 - Army [Image 3]."

201 "7th Conference of the Methodist Church of New Zealand, Christchurch, 27 Feb. - 11 March, 1919."

202 "Rands, The Rev. Frederick," Commonwealth War Graces Commission, accessed July 7, 2015, http://goo.gl/tnyXrE

CONCLUSION

The seven men in this collection represent only the smallest sample of experiences faced by the military chaplain in the First World War. Each of the men recorded herein fought for the man beside him; he sacrificed his safety to recover wounded brothers, to comfort the dying and to keep the men if his outfit moving forward. They were dedicated to God, but also to the King, New Zealand and the individual soldier.

No attempt was made in these biographies to pinpoint the individual *padre*'s level of faith; it also does not attempt to analyse the religious disenchantment experienced by some veterans of the war.[203] Indeed, the heart of this collection is not about religion at all or whether or not the "collapse of spiritual values across Europe in the early 20th century" was part of the war's cause.[204] It is about the men who fought and died in a war not their own, even if they never fired a single shot at the enemy.

These men saw the horrors of the war and lost comrades to shells, bullets and disease. They left their loved ones far behind, never to be seen again, and died - save for Father Dore - on foreign soil. They were members of the New Zealand Expeditionary Force, regardless of where they born, and it was as Kiwis that they died.

---

203 Charles Edward Montague, Disenchantment (New York: Brentano's, 1923), 84-102.

204 Peter Evans, "Faith Tested," The Wall Street Journal, accessed July 12, 2015, http://online.wsj.com/ww1/faith-tested.

www.ingramcontent.com/pod-product-compliance
Ingram Content Group UK Ltd.
Pitfield, Milton Keynes, MK11 3LW, UK
UKHW021051270726
13967UKWH00012B/203